I0149216

DEDICATION:

to the ones that dare to dream.

red Oystor

London | Johannesburg | New York

Richard Mann

PREFACE

Words, words, words. We use them, sometimes we abuse them, but they are the fuel that feeds our desire to achieve more than we ever imagined.

This collection of quotes and thoughts is a celebration of success as much as it is an inspiration for success. Whether success for you means crushing it in business, achieving personal growth, or simply waking up every day with a smile, words have the power to move us toward our goals and dreams. But here's the question—what do you make of success?

How do you define it? Is success having a million dollars in the bank? Is it finding fulfillment in your career or raising a happy, healthy family? Maybe it's something less conventional—perhaps success is simply finding peace of mind, or becoming the kind of person your younger self would be proud of. In reality, success means different things to different people, and that's the beauty of it. The first step toward success is clarity—being clear about what success means to you.

This book is divided into 99 quotes and 8 thoughts, each section aiming to spark something within you—to get you thinking, reflecting, and hopefully acting. But while these words are powerful, they are, at the end of the day, just words.

Success doesn't come from reading a book. It doesn't come from writing down goals or making vision boards, either. All those things can help, but success is rooted in action. It's about turning those words into deeds, thoughts into plans, and plans into reality. So, how does one achieve success? If there's one universal truth in all of this, it's that success requires discipline. You've got to be able to follow through, even when things get tough, boring, or downright uncomfortable.

It's easy to be motivated when you're excited, but true success is forged in those moments when motivation fades, and all you're left with is discipline. It's waking up early when you don't feel like it. It's making that difficult phone call, or finishing the project you started even when inspiration is nowhere to be found.

One of the thoughts in this book talks about success not being an accident, and it's true—success is intentional. It's deliberate. You can't plant a mango tree and expect to harvest apples. What you put in is what you get out. If you want to achieve your definition of success, you need to be deliberate about your actions. It's not enough to want success, you have to actively chase it. You need to be mindful of your thoughts and deliberate about your actions. Think of every small decision as a step on the path to success.

But before you start taking those steps, have you really thought about what you want? A lot of people think they want success, but they're not really sure what that looks like for them. It's easy to say you want to be successful, but unless you've taken the time to clearly define what success means to you, how will you know when you've achieved it? Or worse—what if you chase someone else's version of success, only to find that it doesn't fulfill you? This is where clarity comes in. You need to be crystal clear about what you want, and more importantly, why you want it.

That brings us back to the words in this book. Quotes are fantastic little nuggets of wisdom. They can inspire you, motivate you, and even give you a fresh perspective on life. But they're only as powerful as the actions they inspire. If you read a quote that lights a fire in you, great—but don't stop there. Let that fire fuel you to take action.

Think about the bamboo tree, a metaphor often used to describe success. When you plant a bamboo seed, nothing seems to happen for years. You water it, care for it, and yet, day after day, there's no sign of life. It can take up to five years before the bamboo even breaks through the soil. But when it does, it grows at an astonishing rate—sometimes up to 90 feet in just a few weeks. Success is like that. The years of effort you put in may not yield immediate results, but that doesn't mean nothing is happening. Below the surface, your hard work is laying the foundation for something extraordinary. You just have to be patient and trust the process.

So here's a thought: success isn't some far-off destination, it's a daily practice. It's the little things you do every day—the habits, the choices, the mindset. It's not about being perfect or brilliant or having all the answers.

Success doesn't require you to be a unicorn; it requires you to be a workhorse. You just have to keep showing up, keep doing the work, and keep improving, even when you feel like nothing's happening.

This book is a tribute to that process. It's a reminder that success is less about grand, sweeping victories and more about the small, deliberate actions you take every day. It's about discipline, perseverance, and the courage to keep going, even when the going gets tough.

So, as you flip through these pages, take a moment to reflect on your own journey. What does success mean to you? How are you going to achieve it? And more importantly, what are you going to do today to get one step closer to your goals?

Remember, words are just words unless they're backed by action. Let this book be the spark, but it's up to you to fuel the fire. Success is waiting—now, it's your move.

99

QUOTES &
THOUGHTS ON
SUCCESS

Richard Mann

Richard Mann

Published by RedOystor BX
an imprint of RedOystor Media (Pty) Ltd

visit **www.redoystor.com** for more information
Or contact us at **www.redoystor.com/contact-us**
Cover Design & Layout by **RedOystor Media (Pty) Ltd**

Available on Kindle and other retail outlets

ISBN: 978-0-901648-04-4 (Print)

1

Do it alone.
Do it broke.
Do it tired.
Do it scared.
Just do it!

2

Deep inside you know
you are destined for
Greatness.

3

The more you put in
the work, the closer
you get to your desired
Success.

4

If you treat life like a
Game, you're gonna
get played.

5

Your potential is the seed, and every book you read, every new skill you learn, and every *challenge* you overcome is the sunlight and water it needs to thrive.

6

Never allow a *fear* of failure to prevent you from taking action.

7

Disrespect will close
doors that apologies
can't open.

8

What people say about you is none of your *business.*

9

It is worth knowing that it's better to be the casino and not the gambler; because the 'house' always *wins*.

10

Expect the best but also prepare for the worst.

11

Doing the uncomfortable often leads to *growth*.

"Failure is not the outcome – failure is not trying. Don't be afraid to fail."

– Sara Blakely

THOUGHT

Money, Power, Succ(sex).

Success is a lot like sex—everyone wants it, some have mastered it, and those who don't have it seem to talk about it the most. You know the type, right? The ones who are always this close to landing a massive deal, but somehow they're still living paycheck to paycheck?

It's the same with sex; you'll find that the ones who brag the loudest are usually the ones who get the least. And really, what's the rush? Success, like a good intimate encounter, takes time, patience, and a little finesse. No one wants a wham, bam, thank you ma'am version of success, do they?

Now, imagine if success had a secret G-spot. Everybody's searching for that elusive key to unlock their dreams: the get-rich-quick schemes, the 10 steps to overnight wealth books, the latest podcast where some guy with a Lamborghini and a motivational speaker vibe tells you he's got it all figured out. But here's the thing: like sex, success isn't about discovering some hidden treasure map.

There's no golden shortcut. It's about showing up, putting in the work, and getting just a little bit better every day—like, you know, actually reading those Men's Health or Cosmopolitan articles on how to please your partner instead of just winging it!

If success were truly a quickie, then everyone would be millionaires by now, and we'd all be walking around looking smug with giant "I just made it" grins plastered on our faces. But it's more like a marathon, not a sprint—or, better yet, it's like a relationship.

If you're only in it for the short-term thrills, you're gonna be left unsatisfied, rolling over asking, "Was that it?" But if you're in it for the long haul, you'll find that with a little patience, some elbow grease (and maybe a few awkward moments of figuring things out), success, like sex, gets better with time.

Let's be honest: just like there's an awkward learning curve in sex, there's one in success too. At first, you fumble, you trip over your own feet, and let's not even talk about the questionable decisions you make along the way. But as you go on, you start to figure it out.

You learn what works, what doesn't, and, most importantly, you learn to laugh at yourself in the process. Success is about adjusting as you go, not nailing it on the first try. (Pun intended.)

And don't even get me started on the idea of "success gurus." You know, the ones who claim they've cracked the code, telling you that all it takes is following their unique system. Yeah, sure, buddy—just like the guy who swears he's got the secret to the best sex ever but hasn't had a date in years.

Success, much like good sex, isn't about following some universal formula—it's about knowing yourself, knowing your strengths, and learning from every awkward, uncomfortable attempt that didn't quite go as planned.

Now, if you picked up this book thinking it was a manual on how to have a one-night stand with success, well, let me save you some time—it's not. But hey, if after reading this, success happens to fall into your lap unexpectedly, kudos to you!

Feel free to roll over, smile to yourself, and bask in the glory. Just don't forget to send a thank you note. The truth is, success is more about building something sustainable than it is about scoring some short-term victories.

So, here's a little nugget of wisdom: keep it simple. Don't over-complicate it. Show up, do the work, embrace the awkwardness, and maybe, just maybe, you'll find that success, like sex, doesn't have to be rocket science. Besides, whether we admit it or not, we're all chasing a little piece of that dream. We all want to feel like we've made it, even if we don't shout about it from the rooftops.

At the end of the day, whether you're aiming for success in your career, your finances, or your personal life, remember this: it's all about staying the course, learning as you go, and enjoying the ride. Success, like sex, is best when you're all in, fully present, and not rushing to the finish line.

"It's fine to celebrate success, but it is more important to heed the lessons of failure."

– Bill Gates

12

Stress is the test of ones truest character.

13

If you can't handle
stress, you will never
be successful.

14

Mistakes may *teach*,
but hesitation is often
just a waste of time.

15

Change is
uncomfortable,
that's why it is necessary.

16

Find *joy* in what you have, not just in what you want.

17

More is lost by
indecision than
wrong decision.

18

If you never try, you
never know.

19

Time has a way of revealing the genuine *intentions* of people and situations.

20

If you never *try*.
You never know.

21

If you never fail.
You never grow.

22

Indecision!
Is a decision.

"Great achievers are driven, not so much by the pursuit of success, but by the fear of failure."

– Larry Ellison

THOUGHT

Failure is part of the process.

Let's be honest, failure is like that one persistent ex you just can't shake off. No matter how hard you try to avoid it, it keeps showing up at the most inconvenient times, wearing the same smug grin. But here's the twist—failure isn't your enemy.

It's more like that awkward, unwanted house guest that actually teaches you a few life lessons if you let them hang around long enough. And honestly, failure is part of the process, whether we like it or not.

People love to talk about success like it's a perfectly executed rom-com ending—everything falls into place, and cue the slow clap. But what no one tells you is that the bloopers reel is just as important, maybe even more.

Failure is that scene where you trip over your own feet while trying to look smooth. It's embarrassing, sure, but without it, you're missing out on the lessons that turn you into someone who can actually achieve lasting success.

Think about it—failure is like the universe's not-so-subtle way of telling you, "Hey, buddy, maybe not like that." It's the equivalent of life giving you a facepalm emoji. And guess what? That's okay! Because failure is how you figure out what doesn't work, and in the grand scheme of things, that's pretty valuable information. It's like cooking; the first time you burn the dish, you learn not to set the oven on the temperature of the sun.

Let's get real for a second: we've all heard stories of how wildly successful people failed before they made it big, right? But we're not just talking about small, cute little mistakes—some of them failed spectacularly. Steve Jobs got kicked out of his own company. J.K. Rowling was rejected by 12 publishers.

Thomas Edison failed about 1,000 times before finally inventing the lightbulb. These aren't just mild oopsies; these are epic fails. But that's the point: these failures didn't stop them—they were stepping stones.

So if you fail—and spoiler alert, you will—it doesn't mean the game is over. It means you're playing the game right. In fact, if you aren't failing, you're probably not aiming high enough. Failure is proof that you're pushing yourself, that you're getting out of your comfort zone. And that's where the magic happens, people!

Picture this: You've set out on this grand adventure to scale the mountain of success, and naturally, you're hoping for smooth sailing, right? Wrong! The reality is more like stumbling, tripping, and falling on your face halfway up. But instead of being discouraged, here's the kicker—you dust yourself off and keep climbing, because that's what it takes. The peak is still waiting for you, but you're only going to get there if you accept the falls as part of the process.

And hey, failure even makes for great stories. No one wants to hear about how you nailed everything on the first try. Boring! People want to hear about how you tried to bake a cake, ended up with a fire in your kitchen, but eventually learned how to make a five-layer masterpiece. Failure gives you character. It's like seasoning—it makes everything taste better in the end.

The thing is, failure doesn't define you unless you let it. It's not the end of the road; it's just a pit stop where you grab some snacks and refuel for the next leg of the journey. You're not supposed to camp out there and unpack your bags. You're supposed to learn from it, grow, and then move on. Success is just on the other side of those failures, waiting for you to show up a little wiser, a little tougher, and a whole lot more prepared.

So, next time failure comes knocking on your door, invite it in, offer it a cup of coffee, and take notes. Because that annoying guest? They're actually helping you become the version of yourself who will succeed.

Failure is part of the process—it's the uncomfortable, messy, sometimes hilarious part, but it's necessary. And trust me, when you finally hit success, you'll look back and realize that all those faceplants were worth it.

"The only way to do great work is to love what you do."

– Steve Jobs

23

If you want to be great, learn the habits and *disciplines* of great other people - admire them, emulate their desire and drive, and you will replicate their greatness.

24

Increase your *potential* by setting aside time each week for self-improvement activities.

25

You'll always win when you make the *effort* to do the best you can.

26

Investing in yourself is truly the key to *unlocking* your potential.

27

Your *greatness* knows no bounds when you prioritize personal growth and development.

28

Keep striving for *excellence!*

29

It won't happen
overnight.
But if you quit.
It won't happen at all.

30

Staying *dedicated* and consistent in your efforts leads to eventual success.

31

Achieving meaningful goals takes time and effort.

32

True *progress* hides
in the small repetitions,
revealing itself only
when we show up day
after day.

33

It takes many days,
weeks, months, and
even years to achieve
overnight success.

"The only limit to our realization of tomorrow will be our doubts of today."

– Franklin D. Roosevelt

THOUGHT

Get comfortable with being uncomfortable.

Let's face it, if you want to be successful at anything, you've got to get comfortable with being uncomfortable. Discomfort is like that long-lost best friend who pops up when you least expect them and you feel like you have to explain why your house is not clean when they visit—and trust me, if you want to get anywhere in life, you're going to need to get pretty cozy with doing things that make you squirm a little.

If you wait for the stars to align, for the perfect moment, the right team, and the moon to be in retrograde, you'll still be sitting on your couch wondering why life hasn't handed you success on a silver platter. Newsflash—it doesn't work that way!

Success doesn't send you a formal invitation. Nope, it's more like that friend who shows up at your house unannounced and expects to crash on your couch for a few days. The timing will never feel perfect, the conditions will rarely be ideal, and trust me, the people around you will be far from flawless (you know that friend who never returns your Tupperware? Yeah, those people).

So here's the deal: the right time is now. No, seriously. Right now. Don't sit there overthinking it. If you wait until you feel completely "ready," you'll be waiting until you're 87 years old, wondering where the time went.

There's never going to be a magical moment when you have all the answers or all the tools in your toolbox. Spoiler alert: even the most successful people started out feeling like they had no clue what they were doing. The difference? They started anyway.

Think of it like this: you're standing at the edge of a pool, dipping your toe in the water, waiting for it to feel "just right" before you jump in. But guess what? That pool isn't getting any warmer. You just have to cannonball in, make a splash, and figure out how to swim as you go. Sure, you might swallow a bit of water, maybe even belly-flop, but hey, that's part of the fun. The point is, you started.

Starting before you're ready is like ordering an Uber when you're still in your pajamas. You don't have time to perfect your look, and maybe your hair isn't exactly Instagram-worthy, but you've got places to be, so you just go.

It's not always pretty, but you'll get there. You have to embrace the fact that you're never going to feel like you have it all together—and that's okay. Imperfection is underrated, anyway.

The truth is, people, places, and circumstances are there to teach you lessons, not to be your crutch. You know that saying, "The people you meet will either bless you or teach you"? Yeah, well, sometimes they do both. And sometimes they just irritate you until you realize they're teaching you something important about patience or resilience or whatever lesson the universe is trying to hammer into your thick skull.

So stop waiting for the "right" people to come along. Work with the ones you've got, learn from them, and keep moving.

And while you're at it, stop holding out for the "perfect" place to launch your dreams. Whether you're working from a five-star office with a corner view or from your kitchen table with your cat judging your every move, the point is to start. The world's greatest inventions, ideas, and successes didn't come from waiting around for ideal conditions—they came from rolling up your sleeves, doing the best you could with what you had, and figuring out the rest as you went along.

You know that saying about planting trees? "The best time to plant a tree was 20 years ago. The second best time is now." Well, the same goes for success. The best time to start was yesterday, but if you missed that boat, the second-best time is right now. So stop looking for the perfect day, place, or team. Grab what you've got, dust off your metaphorical boots, and get to work.

Success isn't about waiting for life to hand you the perfect set of circumstances—it's about doing the most with what you have at your disposal. So stop stressing over getting all your ducks in a row. Half the time, they won't even stay in line, anyway. Just dive in headfirst, embrace the mess, and keep moving forward. Because the only thing more uncomfortable than doing the uncomfortable is doing nothing at all.

And if you need a final kick in the pants: You'll never get 14h63, because what even is that? *Exactly*—it doesn't exist!

"Don't be afraid to give up the good to go for the great."

– John D. Rockefeller

34

Progress is *progress*, no matter how small or slow it might be.

35

Where you have no
authority, don't make it
your responsibility.

36

Get comfortable with
the idea of being
uncomfortable.

37

Becoming the best version of yourself comes with a lot of goodbyes.

38

Happiness is a
byproduct of good
habits.

39

Imagination is the *spark* that fuels innovation and progress.

40

There are no ordinary moments!

41

It's not about being 'perfect,' it's about being the best version of yourself.

42

If you don't wake up
and care about your
future, no one else
will.

43

Dream *big*!
Start small.
Make smart choices.
Be consistent.
And anything you want
is possible.

44

Don't settle for good enough.

"The only
person you
are destined
to become is
the person you
decide to be."

- Ralph Waldo Emerson

THOUGHT
It's Not a Destination,
It's a Daily Grind

Okay now. Let me be honest; success is not some vacation spot with a tropical piña colada where you rest after 'arriving.' That seems too good to be true.... Well, sorry. That's not the case. Success is not some magical location to which you can only travel once in your lifetime after you have completed your checklist of all the things you are meant to do in life. It's more akin to an extension of a journey; a knotted road, with some chasms dotting the road and sometimes stopping to reflect upon something to learn from it.

That's not how it works; success is not in possessions – a swanky car, a huge mansion or a yacht which is used only twice in a year (if you are lucky) and only then because it's feared by most or many people. Of course, those things are to be desired. But practical achievement is what was worth, well, it is, who you are during that course.

It is like how the most important thing about a well-built sandwich is the stuffing and not the bread. The bread is fairly simply there to hold all of the appetizing contents together, the more interesting things are in the center – just as on your way to success the only part that really matters is your growth and progress.

Think about it like this: if success was a one-time achievement, some of the most successful people in the world would have gotten bored and checked out ages ago. But they keep going because success is a moving target.

You're supposed to keep evolving, growing, and—get this— sometimes failing. That's right. A bad day, week, or month doesn't mean you've taken a permanent wrong turn; it just means you're human, and that success is as much about the missteps as it is about the big wins.

Success is a verb—a doing word, folks! It's not a trophy you throw on your shelf to collect dust; it's about constantly getting better, even on the days when you feel like you're going backward.

Sometimes, success looks like checking off a big goal, and other days it's just about not giving up when you're ready to toss in the towel. It's about showing up every day—whether it's a triumph or a train wreck—and figuring out how to be better tomorrow than you were today.

So, if you're waiting for success to feel like a glamorous, static achievement, good luck! Success is less about the "stuff" you accumulate and more about the person you're becoming. And, spoiler alert, this version of you is a work in progress (and that's totally okay).

The person you are today is just one version of you, and the person you're becoming? That's a mix of your goals, your dreams, and the effort you put in. But guess what? That doesn't mean you won't have off days, feel stuck, or think you're a million miles away from where you want to be. What it does mean is that every day—good or bad—is part of the bigger picture. Some days are blessings, and some are lessons (and let's be real, sometimes it feels like all lessons and zero blessings, but we move!).

Success is a process, not a personality trait. It's a culmination of who you want to be and the small, daily actions you take toward that.

Think of it like a buffet: it's not about stacking your plate to impress others; it's about choosing what fuels you and keeps you going. So, buckle up, because the ride isn't about reaching a final destination—it's about enjoying the journey and becoming the best version of you, bumps and all.

"The greatest discovery of my generation is that human beings can alter their lives by altering their attitudes of mind."

– William James

45

The *magic* you are looking for is in the work you are avoiding.

46

Being poor is expensive.

47

In order to *change*
your reality, start
by upgrading your
mindset.

48

Upgrade your thoughts
to reshape your world.

49

Focus on your *strengths*; tend to your weaknesses and resist the temptation to be more like others.

50

When your life starts
coming together,
confidence will
develop naturally.

51

Know what you want
and go for it.

52

There is only one person that determines your *success* and that's you.

53

Never let others define your *value* and limit your potential.

54

When you know your *worth*, others see it too.

55

You glow differently when your confidence is built on self-belief and not outside validation.

"The biggest risk is not taking any risk... In a world that's changing really quickly, the only strategy that is guaranteed to fail is not taking risks."

– Mark Zuckerberg

THOUGHT
Embrace Your Inner Weird and Wonderful

Who wants to blend in when you can stand out like a rainbow zebra at a horse show?

Seriously, following the herd is a surefire way to end up like, well... the herd—ordinary, predictable, and probably munching the same grass every day. And comparing yourself to others? Oh boy, you'll either end up feeling vain (like, "I'm totally winning this life game") or bitter (cue: "Why do they have more Instagram followers than me?!").

So, instead of stressing about how you measure up, how about this: own your own weird and wonderful self!

You've got dreams, right? Big, crazy, heart-pounding dreams that make you jump out of bed at 5 a.m. Or maybe 10 a.m.—hey, no judgment here. But those dreams are yours, and chasing them, in your own spectacularly unique way, is the real deal. Sure, some people will think you're odd for not fitting in or playing by the rules.

Newsflash: Steve Jobs literally toasted the "crazy ones" for daring to think outside the box—and let's face it, if you're aiming for real success, you have to be just a little bit nuts. In the best way, of course.

Here's the thing, being different isn't just cool—it's necessary. The people who change the world, who build empires, or even just make their neighborhood a better place—they aren't carbon copies of everyone else.

They're the ones who follow their own paths, make their own rules, and dance to their own beat, even if that dance looks more like awkward moonwalking than a graceful waltz.

We all have our chosen path. And whatever we may think of each other, this life is full of surprises. We learn from each other, walk alongside each other, even though our journeys are different. So don't be afraid to take the unbeaten path. To forge a new way for the next generation.

Look at the evolution of man—had it not been for our ancestors wanting better, we wouldn't be where we are today. Much of what we enjoy, from our freedoms to technology to exploring worlds beyond our own planet, is because someone once thought, "We can do better than that." And they did.

These rule-breakers, adventure-seekers, and creators—what Steve Jobs fondly called "the crazy ones"—were often laughed at for their ideas. But they pursued them anyway.

If not for their daring spirit, we might still be stuck in caves, swiping Tinder on stone tablets. Their courage to be different paved the way for progress.

Here's the thing, being different isn't just cool—it's necessary. The people who change the world, who build empires, or even just make their neighborhood a better place—they aren't carbon copies of everyone else...

So, go ahead. Be inspired by those who've come before you, but don't forget to leave your own footprints on the moon. Because the world doesn't need another "just like everyone else." It needs the wonderfully weird you.

Weird is powerful.

Wonderful is transformative.

And *together*? Well, that's the secret sauce to real success.

You can never conquer the mountain. You can only conquer yourself."

– Jim Whittaker

56

Stand tall.
Believe in yourself.
And let your confidence
shine in *everything*
you do.

57

Nothing and no one can stop you from doing anything you set your mind to.

58

Believe you can, and
you're halfway there.

59

Real confidence isn't just
about feeling superior;
it's about being at *peace*
with who you are.

60

Never let comparison
steal your contentment.

61

Respect the decisions and choices of those with whom you relate. Remember to *honor* their autonomy and individuality.

62

People who motivate and *inspire* us are the ones to keep around. They help us to become the best version of ourselves.

63

Life will test you before
it *blesses* you.

64

The hard reality is that you will never be good enough for the wrong person.

65

Treat people with respect regardless of economic *status*, religious affiliation, or cultural heritage.

66

Take the risk and never
look back.

"Success is not the key to happiness. Happiness is the key to success. If you love what you are doing, you will be successful."

– Albert Schweitzer

THOUGHT
Real Success Takes Time

They say it takes weeks, months and very often years to become an overnight success. Real success doesn't come with shortcuts, fast tracks, or quick fixes. It takes time—lots of it—and patience to match.

Take the bamboo seed as an example. It doesn't sprout for up to 6 months sometimes even up to 5 years; in fact, it stays hidden for what feels like forever. You could water it for months, or even years, and see absolutely nothing. Imagine that, slaving away day in and day out for something that gives you zero feedback in return—talk about testing your faith!

In the case of the bamboo tree, it can take up to five whole years before it even breaks through the soil. Five years of relentless nurturing with no visible sign of progress. You'd be forgiven for thinking nothing's happening down there. Yet, in the fifth year, it suddenly rockets up, growing up to 90 feet in just a matter of weeks! That's right—what took years of unseen effort eventually transforms into something monumental in what feels like no time at all. Success often works the same way: it appears to happen all at once, but in reality, it's the culmination of years of grit, grind, and unseen effort.

If you're sitting there thinking that success will happen in a snap, you're in for a rude awakening. It's going to test your patience, probably to the point of questioning your sanity. Ever felt like you're putting in the work and seeing no results? Well, welcome to the waiting game. The reality is, many of us give up just as we're about to break through that metaphorical soil. We don't stick around long enough to see the payoff because we're trained to expect immediate gratification.

We live in a world where instant is the new norm. Fast food, fast fashion, fast results—you name it, we want it fast. But real success? It's the slow burn. It's like planting a seed, but instead of grabbing your fruit basket right away, you're going to need a shovel, a watering can, and a heck of a lot of faith.

You may wonder, what does a bamboo tree do all those years before it bursts to the surface? Well, it is growing underground! While you may not observe any significant activities taking place on the surface every little seed is putting in place the very core of its explosive system by some climatic conditions extending developing shoots downwards within fertile soil. If it didn't take time to grow those strong roots, chances are, when it finally emerges from the earth with a towering structure, it wouldn't have the strength to support it.

The same phenomenon can be seen with success in whatever area it may be, whether it is your career, personal achievements or your relationships. Everyone has to begin from the bottom up. You have to bury yourself in making the roots if you want to rise to the level of your aspirations. Quite often, people are enamored by the glamorous part of success which is the finished work itself, oblivious to the fact that there are years of unsung hard work, the basis of everything else, that holds the actual work together.

If you've ever been tempted to throw in the towel, remember the bamboo tree. Every drop of water, every shovel of dirt, every bit of sunshine you give it is accumulating into something greater. You're building something that will eventually soar—maybe not today, maybe not next month, but eventually.

That's the beauty of success. It's not just the end result; it's the journey of getting there, the persistence, the small victories, the unseen battles you win along the way.

Now, let's get real—will there be times when you feel like quitting? Absolutely. Will you question why you're even doing this? Definitely. But here's the thing; the moment you break through the soil, it'll all be worth it. You'll look back at those years of toil, frustration, and failure and realize that you were building something monumental.

When success finally arrives, it's not just a reward for your hard work; it's proof of your patience, discipline, and belief in yourself. It validates that the long, challenging journey was worthwhile.

So, the next time you feel like nothing is happening, remember: success requires time. Keep nurturing your bamboo. It may be developing deeper roots, preparing for that incredible growth spurt that will come when the moment is right.

"Success seems to be connected with action. Successful people keep moving. They make mistakes, but they don't quit."

– Conrad Hilton

67

Challenge yourself with *ambitious* goals that push your limits.

68

Set a bar so high most people *think* you're crazy.

69

See failure as a lesson,
when you get rejected,
go again.

70

Rejection is often a form of *redirection*; every 'no' is a step closer to a 'yes', and that's all that matters.

71

How one handles
failures determines
their success.

72

Failure is often an *opportunity* in disguise. Look beyond the perspective of what is, to see what could be.

73

Rejection builds strong character.

74

Success is not a destination, it is the nuggets of moments of *achievement* along the journey.

75

Just because it hasn't
arrived, it doesn't mean
it is not coming.

76

Stay *disciplined* and you'll unlock remarkable growth and potential.

77

Delete everything in
your mind that is not
moving you forward.

"The way to get started is to quit talking and begin doing."

– Walt Disney

THOUGHT

It's never an accident.

Success is like baking a cake. It doesn't just pop out of the oven by accident. You have to follow the recipe, use the right ingredients, mix them in the correct proportions, and bake it at the right temperature.

Now, imagine expecting to get a rich, chocolatey cake by throwing random stuff into the bowl—flour, a bit of ketchup, some pickles, maybe even a shoe. Sounds absurd, right? Well, it's just as crazy to think success happens without deliberate effort and action. You can't plant a mango tree and hope it'll miraculously sprout apples, as much as you may love apple pie.

Jack Dorsey was onto something when he said, "Success is never accidental." It's not a lottery where your lucky numbers happen to hit. Instead, it's a series of intentional actions, decisions, and efforts pointed directly at your goal. Success is a strategy, not an accident.

Everything begins up there in that cranium of yours. You

can't go around with a brain full of distractions and expect to make progress on your goals. Imagine a ship's captain who sets sail without deciding on a destination. He just floats around hoping to bump into an island made of treasure. That's not how it works! You have to know where you're going first—then chart a course.

You've probably heard the saying: "Where focus goes, energy flows." If your thoughts are scattered—one minute, you're thinking about starting a business, the next you're wondering if you left the oven on—you'll end up running in circles. Success requires you to be focused and deliberate in your thinking. Want a thriving business? Imagine it. Visualize the steps. Build it brick by brick in your mind, then go after it like a pirate after gold.

We all want things, right? But wanting something isn't enough. You can't sit around wishing for success like it's the dessert cart at a restaurant. Sure, it's easy to daydream about the life you want—fancy car, beach house, an endless supply of tacos—but what are you doing to make those dreams happen?

Desire isn't just about wanting something; it's about wanting it enough to work for it. It's about aligning your actions with your desires. You can't wish for six-pack abs and then lie on the couch all day binge-watching shows and eating chips. Similarly, you can't expect success to knock on your door while you're busy doing anything but the hard work it requires. Be clear about what you desire and then let that desire fuel your actions.

If thoughts are the spark and desire is the fire, then action is the flame that makes things happen. It's all well and good to have the best ideas and the most burning desires, but if you don't get off the couch, none of it matters. Success requires doing the work—consistently.

You have to be deliberate with your actions. Imagine an artist trying to paint a masterpiece by haphazardly splashing paint on a canvas with no plan in mind. It might be modern art, but it's unlikely to result in the Mona Lisa.

You simply cannot plant one thing and expect something completely different to grow. If you're investing your time and effort in the wrong places, don't expect to get the outcomes you want.

You can't sow negativity, half-hearted effort, or shortcuts and expect to reap genuine success. What you put into your journey feeds your expectations. Want to be successful in your career? Don't spend your evenings scrolling through cat videos and eating snacks. Put in the work, learn new skills, network, and keep moving toward your goal.

Success is a result, not a coincidence. And like baking a cake, if you follow the right steps, you'll get exactly what you've been working toward.

In the end, success is like that delicious cake—planned, mixed, baked, and savored. The secret is to be intentional with every part of the process: from your thoughts, to your desires, to your actions. Every step counts. And the more deliberate you are, the closer you get to savoring the sweet taste of your success.

Remember, no one just stumbles into greatness. Success isn't some magical event that happens overnight while you're sleeping. It's deliberate. It's earned. And with every intentional step you take, you're baking your way toward the life you want—just make sure you're adding the right ingredients!

"If you're not making someone else's life better, then you're wasting your time."

– Will Smith

78

Your *direction* is
more important than
your speed.

79

You get *tested* the most when it's time for you to level up.

80

Anything is possible if you have the *mindset*, the will, the desire to do it, and you put the time in.

81

Adversity creates
opportunity.
To learn.
To grow.
And to *achieve* more.

82

The key to success is to start before you are ready.

83

Success is not final,
failure is not fatal;
it's the *courage* to
continue that counts.

84

Don't wait for success to find you, go out and get it.

85

Success is not about
how high you climb, but
how well you bounce
after falling.

86

The secret to success is *consistency* in your thoughts and actions and a clear focus on your purpose.

87

Success doesn't come from what you do occasionally; it comes from what you do consistently.

88

Success is *simple*: do what's right, the right way, at the right time.

"There are no shortcuts to success, only hard work, commitment, and persistence."

– Gary Vaynerchuk

THOUGHT

You don't have to be brilliant or perfect.

Success isn't reserved for the super-brilliant, the ultra-talented, or those who have their entire lives together in a neat little package with a bow on top. Nope. It's for those of us who wake up, spill coffee on our shirts, forget why we walked into a room, but somehow keep showing up.

Let's be honest; you don't have to be perfect to win at life. You just need to keep putting one foot in front of the other, even if you trip every now and then (okay, maybe a lot).

The idea that you need to be a genius to be successful is a myth, and you need to let go of that idea—ask any of the successful people out there who still don't know how to operate their remote controls. You don't need brilliance, you don't need perfection, just good ol' fashioned effort. You don't have to be a straight A's student, you just need focus and grit.

It's like going to the gym. Sure, there are people who walk in looking like they could bench press a car, but for the rest of us, success means showing up, sweating through the workout, and maybe crying a little on the treadmill. But hey, progress is progress!

You don't have to know everything, be the best, or have it all figured out. Heck, most people don't know what they're doing half the time.

The trick is that they keep doing it. That's the secret sauce. Not some magical formula or hidden gene for genius—just relentless effort. And if you stumble? Good. You're learning. As long as you don't stumble into traffic, you're doing just fine.

Let's face it, perfection is hardly what it is made out to be. If perfection was an essential prerequisite for success, there would probably be three successful people in the entire world—and they would all be robots with a flawless Wi-Fi connection.

True success, which lasts for long, requires one to get their hands dirty, to stay with the messiness of the world. You don't need to ace every test or have a trophy room that looks like a Hall of Fame exhibit. What you really need is to keep showing up and improving, even if you trip along the way.

Success is not about being a unicorn, floating gracefully through life with your glittering mane perfectly in place. It's about being a workhorse. And let's be honest - workhorses have their perks. They are distracted by shiny objects, wander off the road, and may even stop to eat in the grass when no one is looking. But despite the distraction, they keep crawling, step by step, towards the goal, even if the path is bumpy or long.

The truth is that the most successful people I know don't make it to the top because they are super human machines, they get to the top because they self-correct and recover well;

they understand that the road to success isn't one of avoiding failing – because you can't. It's not about being perfect, it's about doing better more often.

You don't have to crush it every single time. What you need is to stay focused on progress, however small it may seem. Being the workhorse means knowing that it's okay to fall down, as long as you get back up and keep going.

Success is not a destination, but a cumulation of efforts, with some winnings sprinkled in between losses and lessons. So drop the need for perfection, and accept your perfectly imperfect self in the pursuit of success.

So here's to the perfectly imperfect, to those who fumble, bumble, and sometimes stumble their way toward greatness.

Keep going, keep growing, and if all else fails, at least you'll have some hilarious stories to tell when you get there!

"To succeed in life, you need two things: ignorance and confidence."

– Mark Twain

89

Success comes to those who are too busy to be looking for it.

90

Success is the art of *believing* in yourself
when no one else does.

91

Behind every success
story is someone who
refused to give up.

92

Success is not defined
by what you achieve, but
by the *obstacles* you
overcome.

93

The road to success
is always under
construction.

Richard Mann

94

Success is the sum of small *efforts*, repeated day in and day out.

95

The only place where success comes before work is in the dictionary.

96

Success is not for the chosen few, but for the few who choose to succeed.

97

Success is not the
destination; it's the
journey.

98

The more you put in the
work, the closer you get
to your desired success.

99

You'll be amazed at
how successful you
can become when you
exercise *discipline* in
all areas of your life.

www.ingramcontent.com/pod-product-compliance
Lightning Source LLC
LaVergne TN
LVHW051413080426
835508LV00022B/3062